Mimi of Nový Bohumín, Czechoslovakia

A Young Woman's Survival of the Holocaust

Fred Glueckstein,
as told by Mimi Glueckstein

Mimi of Nový Bohumín, Czechoslovakia
A Young Woman's Survival of the Holocaust

iUniverse books may be ordered through booksellers or by contacting:

iUniverse
1663 Liberty Drive
Bloomington, IN 47403
www.iuniverse.com
1-800-Authors (1-800-288-4677)

Because of the dynamic nature of the Internet, any Web addresses or links contained in this book may have changed since publication and may no longer be valid. The views expressed in this work are solely those of the author and do not necessarily reflect the views of the publisher, and the publisher hereby disclaims any responsibility for them.

ISBN: 978-1-4502-5009-2 (sc)
ISBN: 978-1-4502-5011-5 (hc)
ISBN: 978-1-4502-5010-8 (e)

Printed in the United States of America

iUniverse rev. date: 4/21/2016

Front cover photograph: Mimi on left, father Max Rubin, and sister Blanka on right.

In memory of Mimi's mother and father, Ernestine and Max, who died in the Holocaust.

Why write memories? Why share experiences?
For the dead, it is too late.
We do all that because it is not too late for our children...
It is never too late.

Elie Wiesel
National Days of Remembrance

Contents

Introduction

At the United Nations on January 27, 2006

"Remembrance and Beyond" was the theme of the first annual International Day of Commemoration to honor the memories of the victims of the Holocaust held at the United Nations on January 27, 2006. It was the sixty-first anniversary of the liberation of the death camp at Auschwitz-Birkenau. For the survivors of the Nazi concentration camps, their children, and grandchildren who came together in the General Assembly Hall on that sunny and chilly day in New York, it was a solemn gathering and a historic event.

The spacious General Assembly was filled beyond capacity with nearly 2,000 people in attendance. As I sat with my mother Mimi, a survivor of the camps like my father Josef who had died in 1999, I thought about the remarkable strength of the survivors, who found the will and courage to build new lives while carrying within them memories of horror, death, and cruelty never witnessed before. As I waited for the program to begin, I wondered how the truth of what happened would be preserved as the dwindling numbers of aged survivors diminish.

With the Holocaust challenged and assaulted by the same forces of ignorance, intolerance, and hate that were the architects of the mass murder, the question of who would tell the story of the Holocaust in the years ahead seemed timely.

The United Nations had stepped forward to help answer that question. In an effort to preserve the memories of Holocaust victims, and to refute those that distorted the truth of what happened, one hundred four sponsors of the General Assembly sponsored a draft resolution by Israel (document A/60/L.12). Dan Gillerman, the Permanent Representative of Israel to the United Nations, introduced the draft resolution. It was the first-ever resolution by that country.

In introducing the draft resolution in October 2005, Ambassador Gillerman said it was imperative for the sanctity of life, for the preservation of humanity, and to prevent atrocities in the future, for all member states to learn the lessons of the Holocaust. The Israeli representative urged the Assembly to adopt the text by consensus so that the United Nations and its members could demonstrate their commitment to the cause with one voice.

The draft resolution designated January 27, the anniversary of the liberation of Auschwitz in Poland by the Soviet Army in 1945, as an annual International Day of Commemoration to honor the memory of the victims of the Holocaust. The resolution also urged member states to develop educational programs "to instill the memory of the tragedy in future generations to prevent genocide from occurring again." Of equal importance, the resolution rejected any denial of the Holocaust as a historical event either in full or in part.

Debate stretched over two days. Representatives from China, Jordan, Guatemala, Republic of Korea, Belarus, Ukraine, Brazil, Argentina, Austria, and the Observer of the Holy See spoke. Delegations expressed support for the historic text, honoring the courage and dedication shown by soldiers who liberated the concentration camps, and commending those countries that worked hard to preserve concentration camps and forced labor prisons used during the Holocaust. While all speakers backed the general content of the resolution, there were calls from the representatives of some delegations, notably Egypt, Malaysia, and Indonesia, to expand the resolution beyond the events of the Holocaust to include subsequent atrocities in the Balkans, Rwanda, and Darfur.

Zeid Ra'ad Zeid Al-Hussein, the representative from Jordan, may have best articulated why the resolution needed to be adopted as introduced. He said there should never be a cessation of relevant lessons drawn from the astonishing and terrifying period of human experience. The Holocaust was a different genocide where wickedness fell into union with human organization. It was a crime of most colossal proportions.

"But to what purpose must we all draw on our memories generally, and, in this instance, the memories of others?" the Jordanian representative asked. "First and foremost, we must of course remind ourselves the extent to which chauvinistic nationalisms or philosophies of negation can be pernicious."

The draft resolution was passed without vote by consensus of the one hundred ninety-one members of the General Assembly on November 1, 2005. The United Nations' historic resolution ensured that the Holocaust and the memory of the millions that perished will be preserved. Among those millions were my grandfather, both my grandmothers, and six uncles and aunts.

As my mother and I prepared to watch the first International Day of Commemoration program in the General Assembly Hall, an old man wearing a dark baseball cap squeezed into the last empty seat in our row. He sat between my mother and a young man in his early twenties, presumably a grandchild of the family members who were seated on the other side of him. The elderly man took off his cap and intently watched the dark-paneled podium with the large symbol of the United Nations on the wall behind it.

I wondered if he was a survivor or there to remember loved ones.

In an elegant voice filled with solemnity and respect, Shashi Tharoor, United Nations Under-Secretary-General for Communications and Public Information, started the ceremony with two minutes of silence to honor the victims. In his remarks, Mr. Tharoor said it was appropriate that the liberation of Auschwitz be commemorated at the United Nations, which was built in the aftermath of the Holocaust.

"When they were confronted by the full horror of what had been done in the death camps of Europe, world leaders were inspired, indeed driven, to create a place where they could work together to change our world for the better," Mr. Tharoor said.

Unable to attend the meeting, then Secretary-General Kofi Annan sent a taped message: "Remembering is a necessary rebuke to those who say the Holocaust never happened or has been exaggerated." Ambassador Ronaldo Mota Sardenberg of Brazil, the acting President of the Assembly also addressed the audience. Ambassador Sardenberg said it was crucial for the international community to remember the horrendous crimes that occurred in Nazi death camps in order to prevent new horrors from occurring in the years ahead. Dan Gillerman, the Israeli representative to the United Nations, gave a speech in which he urged the audience to imagine "the shattering of skulls and the burning of flesh" of the death camps.

After these speeches, Holocaust survivor Mrs. Gerda Weissmann Klein gave an eloquent and moving account of her six-year ordeal. Her trial ended when she was liberated by an American officer named Kurt Klein. Mrs. Klein told of arriving at a former bicycle factory in Volary, Czechoslovakia in 1945 after she and other survivors completed a three hundred fifty mile death march. In a last desperate act to rid themselves of their prisoners, the Nazis locked them in the factory and set a time bomb to kill them all. Miraculously, a rain-storm prevented the bomb from going off.

With the Nazis having fled, the townspeople opened the factory to set the prisoners free. Two days shy of her twenty-first birthday, Gerda was the first to venture outside. She saw an approaching jeep with a white star and two soldiers inside. Wearing a uniform she had never seen before, a tall American officer got out of the jeep and walked toward her. "I weighed sixty-eight pounds. I was in rags. I had white hair," Ms. Klein said. The first words she said to the American were "I am a Jew." The officer responded: "I am a Jew, too." The U.S. Army lieutenant was Kurt Klein, a German Jew who had fled Nazi Germany in 1938. Gerda and Kurt later married.

Mrs. Klein had been introduced by another survivor, Roman Kent, Chairman of the American Gathering of Jewish Survivors of the Holocaust. In his remarks, Mr. Kent noted that it took the United Nations sixty years to have this commemoration. In his rebuke, Mr. Kent related a conversation he had had with his mother long ago as a child. He had told her that she was not beautiful, but she was the only mother he had. Mr. Kent told the audience that similarly, although the United Nations was not pretty, it was the only United Nations we had.

Selected photographs from the Yad Vashem Holocaust History Museum in Jerusalem of some of the victims' infants, children, teenagers, families, and the elderly from Italy, the Netherlands, Poland, Germany, and across Europe, were shown on the large screens. They were the kinds of photographs that every family had in its possession: loved ones captured in a moment of time. Mr. Tharoor, the U.N. Under-Secretary, read the names, ages, and the circumstances of their tragic deaths at the hands of the Nazis. They were poignant, dramatic, and heart-rending photographs of ordinary people in the years before they were innocently pulled into a nightmare unparelled in human history.

The Zamir Chorale of Boston, led by its artistic director Joshua Jacobson, performed a selection of songs from the ghettos and camps. "When I first researched the music of the Holocaust, I was overwhelmed by the sadness and horror," Jacobson recalled in previously published remarks. "Then I learned how prisoners composed ballads to tell the world of the unspeakable crimes they had witnessed and endured. I heard songs that expressed anguish and heartache. And I saw how music sustained hope; how music was the ultimate protest, in some cases the only means of maintaining one's humanity."

The sadness of the Chorale's melodies and haunting refrains filled the cavernous Assembly Hall. Many of the survivors and others in the audience were moved to tears by the music. The program ended with a lecture on the theme "Remembrance and Beyond" by Professor Yehuda Bauer, Advisor to the Task Force for International Cooperation on Holocaust Education, Remembrance and Research. His enlightening and impassioned lecture was the first in a proposed annual series.

The old man in the baseball cap had been crying throughout the program. The young man to his right engaged him in conversation, perhaps to console him. The elderly gentleman showed him the tattoo on his arm the number burned on his flesh by the Nazis. My father had one, too. Of all the images and words shown or spoken that day, the simple gesture seemed for me the most symbolic of the day's theme "Remembrance and Beyond" a survivor of the Holocaust reaching out to a person of a younger generation and showing him what his words could not explain.

The old man's act answered in unequivocal terms the question of what happens after the last of the survivors are gone: it will be left to the present and new generations to see that future International Days of Commemoration at the United Nations, and other similar events around the world, continue. It will be left to them to honor the memories of the victims of the Holocaust, both those that perished and those that survived. They will need to explain, as the General Assembly understood in adopting its historic resolution, how the lessons of the Holocaust must prevent the atrocities of the future.

The question to be asked is: Who will step forward?

Fred Glueckstein
Sykesville, Maryland
2010

Chapter One

Growing Up In Czechoslovakia

In 1938, I was seventeen years-old. I was a slim, dark-haired, brown-eyed young woman. At that time, living in Nový Bohumín, Czechoslovakia (where I was born on September 29, 1921) were some three hundred Jewish families in a population of ten thousand. The official pre-war records listed nine hundred eighty-four Jews, including my parents Max and Ernestine (née Reinisch) Rubin, my sister Blanka, and me. Because of our proximity to Germany, many people in the town, like my family, spoke both Czechoslovakian and German fluently.

One of my fondest memories from before the madness was unleashed, were the delicious Stachelberrn. They grew in the backyard of my grandparent's apartment building, where I lived with my family. The oval, green looking-grapes with stripes, more commonly known as gooseberries, were sweet and aromatic. The Stachelberrn grew on spiny bushes near the nice little garden and cherry tree, alongside another of my favorites, the Ribiseln, or red currants. The fruits grew close to the cottage, near my grandfather's Sukkah, where he took his meals during the Jewish festival of Sukkot.

At that time, Nový Bohumín had three schools in which classes either were taught in Czechoslovakian, German, or Polish. I saw children from neighboring towns each day come from the train station, mainly to attend the German school that was the largest of the three.

Nový Bohumín was a quiet place. We had a tranquil life. My family was neither rich nor poor. We were best described as middle-class, working hard to make ends meet. My circle of friends included girls my age and boys that were slightly older. The residents of Nový Bohumín were good people. There was no anti-Semitism.

The first Jews in Nový Bohumín can be traced to 1655, when the local lord permitted a Jewish soap-maker and a Jewish distiller to live under his jurisdiction. By 1751, six Jewish families lived in various localities of Oderberg, which is the German name for Nový Bohumín. In the early nineteenth century, many more Jews settled in Nový Bohumín. They were attracted to the town because it was one of the important railway-crossings in Central Europe and later the site of an oil refinery. In 1900, a synagogue was built, an independent Jewish community was established in 1911, and a Jewish center opened in 1924. There was also an elementary school. In 1933, a large Maccabiah, or sports festival, was held in Nový Bohumín.

In 1938, my family lived in the center of the city on a street named after Dr. Edvard Beneš, the leader of the Czechoslovak independence movement and the country's second president. We lived with eleven other families in a three-story gray concrete apartment building owned by my grandparents. Our apartment was on a lower floor. As one came in through the front door, there was a bathroom, spacious kitchen, bedroom, and terrace overlooking the backyard. There was also a living room, where Blanka and I slept. Another bedroom, one that was sometimes rented, could be entered through a separate door in the hallway. There was no telephone or radio.

Apartment buildings similar to mine adjoined the building. Shops adorned their front entrances. A movie theater, a cafe, and businesses were across the narrow cobblestone street. Further down the street was a large supermarket named Bachrach after the Jewish family that owned it. Running along Beneš Street was a streetcar that stopped near the front of my apartment building.

My father owned a jewelry business. He had learned to repair watches in Switzerland before his marriage to my mother. Before going to Switzerland, he lived with his sister Caroline in Vienna, Austria. She had four children: Max, Mori, Lottie, and Mali. Their family name was Drechsler.

My father's first jewelry store in Czechoslovakia was located a few streets from where we lived. However, after a burglary in 1937, he moved to one of the two store fronts that were part of the apartment building we lived in on Beneš Street. I worked in my father's shop, which had the family name, Rubin, on the outside. A small window with jewelry on display looked into the store. Although my father wanted me to become a watchmaker, I didn't. Later, I wished I had, as a trade would have been beneficial when times became difficult. However, I closely observed father, and I learned to take a watch apart and reassemble it.

Father enjoyed my company in the store. He would have liked my mother, Ernestine, to spend time in the shop too, but she needed to attend to her mother. My grandmother lived in the same building and was troubled by stomach ailments and very poor vision. Suffering from cataracts, she wore dark glasses that made her look forbidding and unapproachable.

Grandmother was very demanding. Mother attended her most afternoons and evenings. On nice days she took her to the nearby municipal park, where they would sit for hours. The park was an island of respite with dozens of species of bushes and trees ranging from acacia to the northern white cedar. With wide expansive fields of grass, the lovely park was dotted with benches. On warm, sun-filled days, it was crowded with families and young people. Tennis courts and a snack bar with tables and chairs were popular spots. During my free time I enjoyed strolling in the park. I wanted to play tennis, but mother thought I was too thin to play the sport. "Put on extra pounds, Mimi, and you can play tennis," she told me laughingly.

Grandfather, who had died in his sleep a few years earlier, had been a religious man who observed the Jewish holidays. He had written books on the Talmud in Hebrew and spent long hours writing and reading.

The family dinner was usually at 6:00 p.m. Afterwards, Blanka and I met our friends and strolled on the main street. On occasion, Blanka, who was adventurous, and some of the others would walk to the old cemetery after dark. In their game, the person who traveled alone from one side of the cemetery to the other would win ice cream bought by the others. There were also fun times when our cousins, the Perlmans, who lived in the nearby city of Moravská Ostrava, visited us.

The park in Nový Bohumín opened at the far end onto a street and a modern gray school that I attended before graduation. It was called the Gymnasium. Depending on whether a student would go on to the university, he or she would study there for four or eight years. When my friends and I had a break between classes, we would go to the park and talk and laugh among the green and peaceful surroundings before returning to school. It was a pleasant life.

After graduation from the Gymnasium, my older sister Blanka, and I traveled daily by train to a business school in a nearby city, where we learned typing and other secretarial skills. By 1938, I worked in my father's jewelry shop, and my sister worked in the office of a Jewish-owned lumber company. But disturbing events were to take place across Czechoslovakia that would intrude into the idyllic lives of my family.

Chapter Two

Poland and Nazi Germany Invade
Nový Bohumín in 1938 and 1939

On October 2, 1938, Polish cavalry, motorcyclists, and infantry with unfurled flags, massed at the bridge over the Olza River at Teschen, a city on the border of Poland and Czechoslovakia. The Poles carried bayonets, machine guns, and flowers. The bridge had separated the Polish and Czechoslovakian parts of Teschen since January 1919, when Czechoslovakia invaded the area that Poland claimed at the end of World War I. But now, almost twenty years later, Poland annexed Teschen and the surrounding Czech district, including the strategically positioned city of Nový Bohumín where I lived.

As I learned later, the justification for Poland's annexation of the Czech district my family lived in was the Munich Agreement. This pact was signed in the early morning hours of September 30, 1938 by Adolf Hitler, the Austrian-born dictator of Nazi Germany, Neville Chamberlain of Great Britain, Edouard Daladier of France, and Benito Mussolini of Italy. The Munich Agreement called for the Sudetenland, the western regions of Czechoslovakia inhabited mostly by ethnic Germans, specifically the border areas of Bohemia, Moravia, and those parts of Silesia associated with Bohemia, to be evacuated by the Czechs in five stages. In turn, German troops would occupy the Sudetenland. In agreeing to the Munich Agreement, Adolph Hitler pledged peace and an end to territorial expansion.

Winston Churchill, a member of the English Parliament, had stood alone in his concern about Germany's increasing strength. Churchill understood what the Munich Agreement meant. On October 5, 1938, he gave a speech to the House of Commons where he stated the consequences of the Munich Agreement. "We have sustained a total and unmitigated defeat," he told his countrymen. He said all the countries of the Danube valley, one after the other, would be drawn into "the vast system of Nazi politics.' Churchill warned them. "Do not suppose that this is the end. It is only the beginning."

News of the Czech evacuation of the Sudetenland and its occupation by the Germans reached the residents of Nový Bohumín. My father followed the events closely. He read German newspapers like the *Morgen-Zeitung,* which he hid under the table so our Czech neighbors wouldn't see it. They frowned upon other Czechs who spoke German and read German papers. Reports reached Nový Bohumín that the Polish Army had occupied the Czech section of Teschen. Soon rumors spread that Polish troops were heading toward our town.

In the early morning hours of October 9, 1938, Polish troops entered Nový Bohumín. As a youngster, I had no understanding what the occupation of my town by Poland meant for the future. At the time, I was working in my father's jewelry store. Watching the Polish soldiers in Nový Bohumín, I saw young men wearing fatigue caps made of cloth and olive-colored uniforms with black boots. There was no outward display of machine guns or other weaponry. The Poles treated the people of Nový Bohumín politely. They liked spending money in the shops. I served the Polish soldiers who came into the jewelry store to buy my father's watches.

A month after the Polish occupation, the world's focus was on Germany and the Jews. On November 6, 1938, a seventeen year old Jew named Herschel Grynszpan, who we later learned was enraged about his family's harsh treatment and expulsion from Germany, walked into the German embassy in Paris and fired five shots at the first official who would see him.

Three days later, Ernst vom Rath, the junior diplomat shot by Grynszpan, died. Immediately, in retaliation, Nazi storm troopers and Hitler Youth rampaged through Jewish neighborhoods in Nazi Germany and Austria. From November 9-10, the terror and destruction called Kristallnacht, the Night of Broken Glass, saw more than a thousand synagogues destroyed and thousands of Jewish businesses damaged. Thirty thousand Jewish men between the ages of sixteen and sixty were arrested and sent to concentration camps such as Sachsenhausen which was less than ten miles outside of Berlin, the German capital.

Five years earlier on March 22, 1933, the SS (Schutzstaffel), Hitler's "elite guard," established the first concentration camp outside the town of Dachau, Germany for political opponents of the Nazi regime. Between 1933 and 1945, Nazi Germany established about twenty thousand camps to imprison its many millions of victims. These camps were used for a range of purposes including forced-labor, temporary way stations, and as extermination facilities built exclusively for mass murder. By 1934, the SS had taken over administration of the entire Nazi concentration camp system.

Meanwhile, news of the terror of Kristallnacht, and the treatment of the Czech Jews in the Sudetenland, reached my family and other Jews of Nový Bohumín. I could hear father telling mother that the danger was coming closer and closer. "But we will be safe," he told her, "as long as the Polish troops are here and protect Nový Bohumín from the Germans." However, the protection offered by the Poles was not to last. Within one year the Germans had replaced the Poles, and my family, as well as the other Jews of Nový Bohumín, faced the danger firsthand.

On March 15, 1939, within a year of the Germans occupation of the Sudetenland, German troops occupied Prague, the country's capital. They also took control of the western provinces of Bohemia and Moravia which they established as a German Protectorate. Seeing that Hitler had not kept his promise to end territorial expansion, both England and France issued a mutual defense guarantee to all the central European countries between Germany and the Soviet Union.

Less than six months later, at twelve noon on September 1, 1939, the German Army, entered my city of Nový Bohumín. From the window of our apartment, mother, Blanka, and I watched the soldiers marching and singing below us on Beneš Street. In the hours preceding the Germans arrival, the Polish troops had evacuated the town. As father watched the soldiers leave, he knew that every male Jew in Nový Bohumín faced immediate danger with the imminent arrival of the German troops. Father had heard how Jews had been treated by the Germans after they occupied Austria in March 1938. On the first night of the German Anchluss, or annexation, the Germans looted Jewish apartments and stole valuables, pieces of furniture, and art. Austria's Jews, some one hundred eight-five thousand, were singled out for beatings and public humiliations such as scrubbing the streets of Vienna.

Father was well aware that the Nazis would soon launch an operation against the Jews in Nový Bohumín. He knew that the occupation of the Sudetenland had led to the arrest of Jews and Synagogues were torched.

Thus, with only hours of the Germans expected arrival, father and other Jewish men decided that it was prudent to leave Nový Bohumín. But the families were to stay behind.

"It is a hard decision," father explained, "but Jewish women and children will be of no use to the Germans. You will be safe. The others and I will travel east into Poland away from the Germans, find work, and send for you. Is there any other choice?" he asked. On the morning of September 1, 1939, father packed a small valise with clothes, rings, watches, and other jewelry from the shop. Only the clocks on the wall, which had been for sale, remained. The familiar *'tick-tock' 'tick-tock'* of the clocks was the last sounds father heard as he closed the shop for what would be the final time. I was sad to see him leave. A feeling of ill-boding gripped me. And I was right.

I never saw father again.

Unbeknownst to father and his fellow travelers on the day they left, September 1, 1939, Germany mounted an all out attack, or Blitzkrieg, on Poland. With their superior firepower, the German troops overran the western part of the country. The German Air Force, or Luftwaffe, bombed the major cities and key Polish military and civilian installations. We later learned that father's train was bombed by the Germans in an aerial attack. He was unhurt and managed to get to Kraków, one of the largest and oldest cities in Poland. Kraków is located in the southern part of Poland, on the Vistula River in a valley at the foot of the Carpathian Mountains. There he melted into the city, which was seized by fear and nervousness.

On September 3, 1939, two days after the attack on Poland, Great Britain and France declared war on Germany. The Second World War began. Meanwhile, German forces advanced across Poland. On

September 6, Hitler's troops occupied Kraków, and about sixty-thousand Jews came under Nazi authority. Father was trapped.

Meanwhile, in Nový Bohumín, the Germans took over the city hall and police station using these facilities as their headquarters. There was looting by the soldiers, and father's shop was vandalized. Uneasiness fell over the Jews. The Germans used selected Jews to communicate with the other Jewish residents. One day, Blanka, my friends, and I were told to report to German headquarters, where we were registered and immediately assigned work. The Germans were interested in people capable of working. Elders like mother and grandmother were exempt. Men and boys were put to work rebuilding a bridge blown up by the Poles.

A number of young women and I were assigned to work at the Army barracks just outside the town where the German soldiers were housed. I was given housekeeping chores. Each day the others and I met at Nazi headquarters and walked, sometimes with a German guard, about forty-five minutes to the barracks. There another guard supervised our work. I scrubbed the toilets and swept the floors. And after a full day of work, I trudged back to Nový Bohumín. The situation for the Jews of Nový Bohumín soon worsened.

I saw the fire from my window. The synagogue was in flames. It was September 23, 1939 and the Jews of Nový Bohumín were observing Rosh Hashanah, or the High Holy Days. The Germans knew the special significance of Rosh Hashanah for the Jews and deliberately set fire and destroyed synagogues across Poland.

Six days later, I turned eighteen-years-old. Two months after that, on November 23, 1939, some seven weeks after Germany's invasion and occupation of western Poland, all Jews appearing in public over the age of ten were ordered to wear white armbands. The armband had to be at least four inches wide, and had to display in blue the Jewish Star of David. The Germans decreed that the armband was to be worn on the right sleeve of all inner and outer garments. Failure to wear it was punishable by death. The armband was another form of public humiliation. People on the streets in Nový Bohumín stared at the Jews. The Germans watched us closely, and I took every opportunity to avoid them.

Later, I was assigned to work at the hospital in the old section of Bohumín. Walking there from where I lived brought back memories of a happier time. Before the occupation, Blanka, our friends, and I would walk to the city's old section to bathe in the swimming pool. It was a small pool called Spuckestel. It was located at the far end of town on a big piece of land. From the swimming pool I could see the Oder River. And across the river were the rolling hills of Germany.

Chapter Three

Transported to the Polish Ghetto of Będzin

The hospital in the old section of Bohumín was a large and well-known building. When I started working there, it struck me as odd that it was empty. All the patients were gone. On each floor there were empty corridors and unused beds. It was quiet and eerie. While working in the hospital, I washed windows, scrubbed floors, and cleaned mattresses. What happened, I wondered, to the patients that had occupied the beds? Where were the doctors and nurses? What did the Germans plan to do with the hospital? My questions went unanswered.

Some moments in life are never forgotten. One of those times began with a knock on the door of our apartment. When I opened the door, I was gripped by fear. Two German soldiers faced me. One was an officer. The Germans came in uninvited. They inspected the bedrooms, kitchen, and living room, where the officer came across a sparkling crystal bowl sitting atop a table. The bowl was a favorite of mother. The officer ordered the soldier to take it.

Other items may have been taken from the apartment that day, but the loss of the crystal bowl stayed with me. Hadn't the Germans already caused my father to leave, stripped me of my liberty, and assaulted my dignity by forcing me to wear an armband. They then came into my home and took what they wanted. What else were they capable of doing? I wondered? I soon found out.

I don't remember when I first heard the terms Judenfrei and ghetto, but I soon understood what they meant. Judenfrei was the German word for an area free of Jewish presence. It meant that a place like Nový Bohumín would be free of its Jewish residents. Ghettos, which were established by the Germans after the invasion of Poland, were intended to segregate Jews from non-Jews. In early 1940, mother, grandmother, Blanka, and I received word we were to relocate from Nový Bohumín to southern Poland. The news was expected. We had heard for some weeks from the Jewish community that all the Jews would be sent to one of two cities.

We were being sent to a town called Będzin (*Bendzin* in German). In the years before the German invasion of Poland in 1939, Będzin had a vibrant Jewish community. From the beginning of the seventeenth century, a Jewish settlement existed there. The Jewish population in Będzin was considerable, and by 1931 it numbered 21,625, or 45.4 percent of the population. During the 1930's, Będzin was a center for Zionism, an international political movement that supported the reestablishment of a homeland for the Jewish people in the historic land of Israel. Prominent figures from the World Zionist Movement visited Będzin.

The German occupation of Będzin, Poland took place on September 4, 1939, and the Germans renamed it Bendsburg. Five days later, the German Army burned the Great Synagogue in the Old City. Two hundred Jews were locked in the synagogue when it was set on fire. Anyone trying to escape the burning building was shot dead. These massacres happened again and again across Poland.

Afterward, several thousand Jews from the district were expelled and forced to reside in Będzin. A Judenrat, an administrative body that the Germans required Jews to form, was established in the early stages of the occupation. The Judenrat served as a liaison between the German authorities and the Jewish communities under occupation. The Judenrat operated the area's pre-existing Jewish communal properties, such as hospitals, soup kitchens, day-care centers, and vocational schools. It was against that backdrop that mother, grandmother, Blanka, and I found ourselves packing to relocate to Będzin. We were able to take a few possessions: a bed, a table, and a clothing closet. The items were picked up by some Jewish workers and taken to the train station for shipment to Będzin.

It was strange to be leaving Nový Bohumín. It was the only home I had known. The four of us took the train to Będzin, where a member of the Judenrat met us. We were told that our apartment was not ready and that we would stay with some Jewish families at first. Blanka and I stayed with different families. Mother and grandmother remained together. After a week, we moved into the apartment on the outskirts of Będzin, which was a short walk into the city itself. The apartment building was relatively new. There were three or four other tenants.

Będzin was an open ghetto. Unlike a closed ghetto, it had no walls or fences, but there were restrictions on entering certain streets and shops. Jews wore armbands. Grandmother did not fare well in Będzin. The travel to a new city had taken a toll on her health, which deteriorated. Mother took care of her as well as she could, but the lack of medicine was a problem. When Blanka heard there was a doctor living nearby, she went to see him. Blanka asked the doctor, who was a non-Jew, if he could see our grandmother. The doctor refused. Grandmother slipped into a coma and died.

While we struggled to survive in Będzin, German officials in Berlin were conferring on the fate of the millions of Jews in Europe. In 1940, a decision was made to establish a new camp for Polish political prisoners in a place in southern Poland. The Germans named the town Auschwitz. Prisoners at Auschwitz were used as slave laborers by fifty-one German companies such as I.G. Farben, and international companies as well, including the Ford Motor Company's German operations. The complex at Auschwitz would eventually expand to three camps. In the summer of 1941, Rudolf Höss, Auschwitz's commandant, was ordered to Berlin, where he was given orders to begin the systematic extermination of Jews.

Höss was told that Auschwitz was chosen for this purpose because of the size of the camp, its isolation, and its railway links with lines across Europe. Höss needed a method to kill Jews. After considering options, he decided on Zylon B, the trade name for a form of cyanide known as hydrocyanic acid. Zylon B was used commercially to kill rats. By late 1941, work began on Auschwitz II near a village named Birkenau, Three gas chambers, capable of handling one-thousand people, were built. Arriving Jews entered a small iron gate topped by a sign that read *"arbeit macht frei"* (work makes you free). After men, women, and children were gassed, the dead corpses were removed and taken to crematoriums, where the bodies were burned. Jews across Europe knew about Auschwitz.

What would not be known until after the war was the scope of the killings at the infamous death camp. The number of people who perished at Auschwitz between 1941 and 1945 were some one and a half million. Most of the people killed by the Germans were Jews.

Meanwhile, Blanka found a job teaching German to a child of a Polish family in the nearby town of Sosnowiec. As Będzin was an open ghetto, she was allowed to travel regularly to the town. Blanka took the streetcar but was required to travel in the last car, which was red and designated for Jews only. One day, we received word that father was alive and living in Kraków. Blanka decided that she had to see him. She told mother and me of her plan. "As I don't look Jewish," explained Blanka who was fair skinned, had light colored hair, and spoke German. "I will take off my armband and travel to Kraków by train. I know someone who will give me a pass to travel."

Despite our grave reservations, Blanka was determined to go. Blanka traveled from Będzin to Kraków by train. Upon reaching her destination, she hailed a *droshkie*, an open four-wheeled horse-drawn passenger carriage that served as local transportation. Blanka asked the driver if he knew the section of the city where the Jews lived. He said he did, and Blanka found father. After a tearful reunion, they brought each other up to date. When he heard of our plight in Będzin, he wanted to return with Blanka. But it was impossible for him to leave Kraków.

Before Blanka left, father gave her a ring that he had taken with him from the jewelry shop when he left Czechoslovakia. "The ring has a diamond and it has value," he said. "It should help buy food for your mother and Mimi." Blanka was reluctant to take it, but when he insisted she sewed into the lining of her coat for protection. Blanka bade him a sad farewell. She would never see father again.

Years later, we learned about his fate. On March 13-14, 1943, the Nazis carried out the final liquidation of the Kraków ghetto. Eight thousand Jews deemed able to work were transported to the Plaszow labor camp. Those deemed unfit for work, some two thousand Jews, were killed in the streets of the ghetto. Others were sent to Auschwitz.

As part of the liquidation of the ghetto, father was moved east to a Polish town believed to be Brzozów which was close to the Soviet Union.

In late 1944 or early 1945, with the tide of the war having turned against Germany, the German guards told father and the other prisoners that they were freed. The prisoners were pointed in the direction of a forest. On the other side, they were told, was the Soviet Union. Father and the others left the camp and walked into the forest believing that freedom was a short distance away. But waiting in ambush were SS troops, who executed father and the others.

Chapter Four

Mother Is Sent to Auschwitz

After seeing father, Blanka returned to Będzin without incident. She gave mother the ring, but mother didn't know what to do with it. She put it away, but it was never used as father intended, and I don't know what happened to it. Meanwhile, we adjusted to life in the ghetto. Blanka found a job in a garment factory. One day she did not return home. Mother and I were frantic. Neighbors told us that Blanka had been taken by the Germans in a roundup, which occurred from time to time when able-bodied Jews were needed by them for forced labor.

I learned later that Blanka was crying and shaking as she was loaded into an old truck with others who had been randomly pulled off the street. Blanka believed that she would be killed. While Blanka trembled with fear, the Germans told her that she was in no danger, as she and the others were needed to work. Blanka found herself in a forced labor camp for Jews at St. Annaberg in Germany; the first of four concentration camps she would be imprisoned in.

In Będzin, mother and I were deeply shaken by Blanka's abduction. We were fearful of what the future held, but the future soon arrived. We were notified that the Jews of Będzin were being relocated to the nearby town of Kamionka, a closed ghetto that from which Jews were not allowed to leave. If a Jew left the ghetto without permission, he or she was killed. Mother and I were assigned an apartment in a building that was a two-floor walk-up. We shared this apartment with another couple, a husband and wife, from our hometown of Nový Bohumín. The building was in an undesirable part of Kamionka, where people in the best of times did not venture.

The conditions were very bad. Our only water source was a pump across the street from the building, from which we carried water up to the apartment. There were no bathrooms, and we had to use a communal outhouse. Adding to the misery was the curfew. No one was allowed to leave the apartment building after 8:00pm. To make money and supplement the ration stamps we were given by the Jewish community, I took a job in a factory. The Allegemeine Schneiderwerkstädte repaired uniforms of German soldiers. I sewed on buttons and mended shirts and pants. It was tedious work but it paid a salary.

I earned twelve German marks a week. Bread on the black market cost nineteen.

One day, mother and I had a visitor from the nearby ghetto of Sosnowitz, which was accessible to Kamionka by crossing a few open fields. Her name was Dela Reich. Dela was an older woman with gray hair. We learned she was a widow. Dela had been informed that her son Fritz was in a forced labor camp in Germany at a town called Sagan, and that he was friends with Blanka. She explained that her son Fritz was a "Juden Elder," or a Jew designated by the Germans to oversee the Jewish prisoners. Because of Blanka's fluency in German, Fritz had gotten her an administrative job in the camp.

Mother and I were relieved to hear that Blanka was alive.

The Gestapo, an acronym for Geheime Staatspolizei meaning secret state police, often came unexpectedly into the Kamionka ghetto where we lived. The Gestapo looked for Jews to transport to forced labor camps. When word reached us and the others that the Germans were coming, we hid in the cellar of the building. Huddled in the dark were men and women, including young mothers and children. Above our heads we could hear the Germans walking on the steps. When they left, we returned to our apartments to spend another night in worry and fear. But in the end there was no escape.

It was now 1943, and one day, the Germans ordered the Jews of the Kamionka ghetto to gather on an open field of grass. This was known as an *Aktion,* or an assembly, for the purpose of deporting Jews to concentration or death camps. Men, women, and children stood all day as a light, steady rain fell. Soldiers guarded us. Night came and nothing happened. We grew tired and sat on the wet grass. Mother and I were frightened.

The next morning the Gestapo ordered the exhausted group of Jews to pass in front of them. As the men, women, and children walked by, the Germans selected some to remain in the ghetto for forced labor. Others were picked for transport to the Auschwitz death camp.

A person's age and physical condition were the basis for staying or being sent to a certain death. I was to remain at Kamionka. Mother was selected for Auschwitz. As mother was escorted with others to a truck, I was upset and very afraid. One by one my family had disappeared: first father was forced to flee, grandmother died, Blanka was taken off the street, and now my poor mother was being sent away.

I was alone. Afterward, I returned to the apartment and sat on my bed. I stared at mother's empty cot and thought about her. Suddenly, there was a series of loud knocks on the door. Opening the door, I was shocked to see mother accompanied by other Jews that I knew. It was a miracle. The men helped mother inside and left quickly. After I got her a glass of water, I asked what had happened. Mother explained that she and the others were driven to what she thought was a school. She had been so afraid and nervous that she had fainted inside the truck. When they were ordered out of the vehicle, she had been left behind in the confusion. While the others were being accounted for by the Germans, people who knew mother had gotten her out of the truck and helped her home. It was a brave gesture by people that risked their own lives.

Exhausted by the events of the day and the preceding night on the wet field, mother fell asleep. I looked at her and was overjoyed to see her, but I was worried about what would happen next. A few weeks later, the Germans liquidated the Kamionka ghetto. At 5:00 a.m., we were ordered to assemble on a wide street. The nightmare of another *Aktion* took place. More than a thousand people were forced to walk in front of the Germans. People were ordered to the right or the left. What happened next was expected. Mother and more than a thousand other men, women, and children were selected and sent to Auschwitz.

It is very hard to think about what happened to mother. Eyewitness accounts of survivors present a picture of a nightmare from Dante's *Inferno*. Henick Sztarkman, a Jew from Radom, Poland, was sent with his mother to Auschwitz. Men and women were separated at the railroad station in their town and loaded into closed cattle cars. It was the last time Heniek saw his mother.

The train reached Auschwitz at dawn. "In a charged atmosphere of the SS cracking whips and shouting '*Raus Juden!*' and driving them on with the butts of the guns," the Jews were pulled out of the train. "Everything took place in an atmosphere of shouting," Sztarkman remembered, "and occasionally a shot is fired and a body falls down just to create this atmosphere of fear and apprehension and compliance ... Prompted by gun butts and kicks, we're unloading quickly and lining up right on the siding in front of the car. The selection on who lived and died was done there. The SS officer started going through the ranks, looking at us and directing us, 'left, right; left, right.' The lucky ones lived and were sent to forced labor camps. Others like my mother were gassed and cremated."

Elie Wiesel, Nobel laureate and Auschwitz survivor, wrote: "Never shall I forget that night, the first night in camp, which has turned my life into one long night, seven times cursed and seven times sealed. Never shall I forget that smoke. Never shall I forget the little faces of the children, whose bodies I saw turned into wreaths of smoke beneath a silent blue sky."

On the day my mother was selected for transport to Auschwitz, I was told to return to our apartment, where two other young people joined me. We knew that we would be sent to a forced labor camp. Later that day, I heard the sounds of children crying on the street. Looking out the window, I saw three children, each between five-and-six-years-old, holding hands and walking down the street. They were crying for their parents. It was a heart-rending sight.

And it would be etched in my memory forever.

Chapter Five

Imprisoned in the Sagan and Blechhammer Concentration Camps

While waiting for news of my transport from Kamionka, I thought about my sister Blanka. Having no one else in the world now but her, I went to see the Judenrat, which was responsible for compiling the list of Jews for transport to the forced labor camps. I asked to be sent to Sagan, where Blanka was last known to be.

The Jewish official said he would do what he could. Shortly, thereafter, another young Jewish woman and I were on a train to Sagan, Germany. The woman's husband was a prisoner there. We were guarded by a soldier with a rifle.

As the train crossed into Germany, I looked at the countryside and worried about the future. I was twenty-one-years-old and scared. Sagan was one hundred miles southwest of Berlin. Later, I learned that the first mention of Sagan as a forced labor camp for Jews had been in February 1941, when one hundred female prisoners worked in the Gebrueder Hoffmann cotton mill. Sagan was also the location of the Stammlager Luft #3, or Permanent Camp for Airmen, a prisoner-of-war camp that housed allied air force servicemen.

When my travelling companion and I arrived at Sagan in April 1943, barbed wire enclosed the camp. It had expanded from its early days and housed both male and female prisoners. My first impression was that the camp was orderly and well-kept. It was small with barracks for the prisoners and the soldiers. Between the barracks was a kitchen building. Pretty flowers were planted out front.

Upon my arrival, I was overcome with joy to see Blanka. We told each other about what had happened since Będzin. I was surprised to again meet Dela Reich, who had visited mother and me in Kamionka. Dela was also successful in being transported to Sagan, where she was reunited with her son Fritz. During the day at Sagan, I sewed clothing. After dinner, we were permitted to walk around the camp and talk with the others. We wore our regular clothes. Blanka introduced me to Fritz Reich. He was a tall, good-looking young man, who was an attorney before his imprisonment. It was clear that Fritz and Blanka were close. I thought Blanka and Fritz would marry one day, but we all had to survive first.

While in Sagan, I learned that a young man I knew from Nový Bohumín was very ill in the infirmary. He was from a well-respected family. I went to visit him but never learned what happened to him, because I was not in the camp much longer.

After about three weeks, the German official who was responsible for a network of forced labor camps, including Sagan, visited the camp. The Lagerführer, or camp commandant, told the official that since his last visit, the camp had new prisoners, including myself and the young woman I had travelled with on the train. The next morning at an assembly of the prisoners, the German official informed me that my travelling companion and I would be sent to another camp the next day.

We were told that regulations did not allow family members to be in the same forced labor camp. That evening, I had a tearful parting with Blanka, Fritz, and Dela. I didn't expect that I would ever see them again. Sadly, the next morning, the two of us were again on a train guarded by a soldier.

I had no idea where the train was headed.

Later I heard that Blanka, Dela and the other women in Sagan were transported to other concentration camps. Sadly, the men, including Dela's son Fritz Reich, were killed by the Germans. Meanwhile, I arrived at the Blechhammer concentration camp located near the Polish town of Kozle. Blechhammer had opened a year earlier as a labor camp for Jews. The original three hundred fifty prisoners had built a synthetic gasoline plant for the Oberschlesische Hydriewerke AG (Upper Silesia Hydrogenation Works). After one hundred twenty of the prisoners contacted typhus, they were sent to Auschwitz, where they were killed. In June 1942, the remaining prisoners were transferred to a new and larger camp built nearby.

By the time I arrived at Blechhammer, the number of inmates had swelled to fifty-five hundred, mostly Jews from Upper Silesia, but there were also Jews from fifteen other countries. On the day that I came to Blechhammer, hundreds of other Jews from all over Europe also arrived by train. The Gestapo gathered the small children and locked them in a laundry room. They were destined for Auschwitz. Their parents were designated for forced labor. The children cried and screamed. A few of the mothers asked the guards to be with their children. These women accepted their fate as they and their children were to go to their death in Auschwitz. It broke my heart.

After a day or so, I was transferred to the main camp or Judenlager, which was divided into two parts. The larger section contained separate wooden barracks for the prisoners. I was one of some two hundred women put into a separate part of the camp. The conditions were very bad. There were no toilets or washing facilities. Hunger, illness, and disease were prevalent, especially diarrhea and tuberculosis.

The camp for the Germans adjoined the prisoners section; a metal gate and an entry door separated the two camps. When it was learned that I spoke German fluently, I was assigned with another woman to spend each day in the German quarters, where I worked in the canteen. I gave the soldiers blankets, soap, and other toiletries. At times, I was told to clean the room of the high-ranking German officer that visited Blechhammer every few weeks to inspect the camp. With a guard watching me, I swept the room and cleaned the windows, but I was ordered not to touch the bed.

Each morning, the Jews assembled outdoors before the Germans to begin the workday. One day, as was usual, most of the prisoners were marched out of the camp to work on the new Autobahn, or automobile highway, while others like me reported to our places of work inside the camp. Between our camp and the Autobahn site was a camp for Allied prisoners-of-war, who were sympathetic to the Blechhammer Jews. At the end of one workday, an Allied soldier passed a can of beans to a prisoner that passed. A guard saw what happened, and the prisoner was dragged to a room in the German section, where I worked. German soldiers savagely beat the prisoner. It was difficult to watch. I felt very bad for him but was powerless to do anything. Afterwards, I was ordered to clean up the room that included the beans that were spilled all over the floor.

The indignities that the Germans imposed on the Jews had no limits. A Jew from Vienna named Karl Demerer served as the "camp elder". In various instances, he stood up to the camp authorities and helped the other prisoners. But his intervention was not always successful. I remember Yom Kippur, the holiest day of the Jewish year, fell on

October 8, 1943. That day is commemorated with a twenty-four hour fast. On that day, I remember the Germans set up picnic tables outside the kitchen where we ate. Each prisoner was forced to eat under the watchful eyes of the guards. There would be no fasting by any devout Jews in Blechhammer.

On a lighter side, on Saturday nights, the camp officials allowed the prisoners to assemble and put on shows to entertain each other; it was one of the few times that men and women prisoners could be together. These shows were held in the sewing room, a large space that could accommodate many people. I remember how talented the people were. They sang and danced. It was a nice escape from the fear, illness, and death that was daily life in Blechhammer.

It was at one of the shows that I met a German Jew named Josef Glückstein.

Chapter Six

Meeting Josef Glückstein

Josef Glückstein was from Kitzingen, Germany, a town in the German state of Bavaria. Surrounded by vineyards, the district of Kitzingen was the largest wine producer in Bavaria and a major center for the wine trade. When I became acquainted with Josef at Blechhammer, he was thirty-years-old. Born on November 21, 1912 to Ferdinand and Esther Rachel (née Markowitz), he was one of ten brothers and sisters. Josef's father, a shoemaker by profession, died of natural causes in 1937.

Being a Jew in Germany was difficult after Adolph Hitler became chancellor in January 1933. The virulent anti-Semitic attacks on the Jews were unrelenting. The most vicious anti-Semitic newspaper was *Der Stürmer*, which was founded and published by a prominent Nazi named Julius Streicher. In a heroic act of bravery, Josef and his brother Moritz waited at the train station in Kitzingen for the delivery of *Der Stürmer* and bought every copy, which the brothers destroyed.

For two weeks in March 1933, Josef was imprisoned in his hometown of Kitzingen by the Nazis and then again for one week in Neuss on the west bank of the Rhine opposite Dusseldorf. Five years later, Nazi storm troopers and Hitler Youth retaliated against the Jews on Kristallnacht, the Night of Broken Glass. At that time, Josef, who worked as a salesman for a Jewish wine company named Fromm, was in the German city of Dusseldorf. When the rampaging on the streets began and the main synagogue burned, Josef decided that the best place to escape to was the railroad station, where among the hustle and bustle, he blended into the crowd.

His quick thinking helped him avoid arrest.

Later the Jewish wine company Josef worked for was confiscated by the Nazis and its owner, Paul Fromm, left for the United States. With the situation deteriorating in Germany, Josef was forced to flee, sadly leaving his mother and sister Berta behind. With forged travel documents, Josef left Germany by bus for Belgium, a neutral country, in 1939. At the German border guards checked each passenger. One guard checked Josef's document and looked at him closely. Josef had blue eyes, blond hair and was fair skinned. The guard decided he wasn't Jewish, and he moved on. The bus proceeded into Belgium and went on to Brussels.

In May 1940, the Germans invaded Belgium and Holland. Josef was arrested in Brussels and on September 11, 1942 he was transported to the eighteenth century barracks at Dossinkazerne in Malines, halfway between Brussels and Antwerp. From Sammellager Malines, as the German called the assembly camp for Jews, Josef was sent in late September 1942 to the Blechhammer concentration camp, where I met him for the first time after I arrived in April 1943.

Unbeknownst to Josef at the time, the Gestapo had taken his mother Esther (born August 20, 1869 in Oswiecim, Poland) into custody. On Rosh Hashanah, September 11, 1942, she was transported (number II/25-948) from Muenchen, Germany, to the Theresienstadt

Czechoslovakia ghetto. (When the Nazis annexed Bohemia-Moravia in my home country of Czechoslovakia in March 1939, the Germans needed additional prison space. Over a year later, on June 10, 1940, the Prague Gestapo converted the Kleine Festung, a small star-shaped fortress in Terezin, into a main concentration camp. Located forty miles northwest of Prague, the Nazis had various names for the camp.) In November 1941, Theresienstadt itself became a major transit camp to Auschwitz and other death camps.

During the summer of 1942, transports began of Jews, many of whom were elderly, from Germany to Theresienstadt. Josef's mother arrived in September with more than twelve thousands others. Overall, more than fifty-eight thousand Jews were crammed into the camp, the highest recorded number of its existence. Hunger, measles, scarlet fever, and tuberculous were rampant. Between 1941 and 1945, 139,654 people were sent to Theresienstadt. Precise German records show that the number that died in the ghetto was 33,430. The number transported to the death camps totalled 86,934.

A young countryman of mine from Czechoslovakia, Egon "Gonda" Redlich, was in Theresienstadt when Josef's mother arrived. Redlich was in charge of youth welfare. Sadly, of the more than fifteen thousand children sent to Theresienstadt barely one hundred survived. Redlich, his wife, and their young son would eventually be sent to Auschwitz and killed, too.

In 1967, Redlich's diary was discovered in an attic in the former ghetto. On September 5, 1942, six days before Esther Glückstein left Germany, Redlich wrote: "The number of dead: one, then ten. After that tens, fifties, sixties. The number grew and grew. It became nearly 100 a day. Now it has reached 130. It's hot here, as it never was before, and there is no one to dig graves. The struggle for life here is immense." In his diary entry of September 20, 1942, Redlich wrote: "A blind woman has been registered for a transport. She has been sitting without help for many hours. They are bringing her to the attic. A small child, ten years old, helps her. A spectacle not to be believed. Anyone who has not seen it would not believe."

The ordeal of travelling had been too much on the health of Josef's mother, Esther. She died in Theresienstadt on Yom Kippur, September 21, 1942, ten days after she left Germany. She was seventy-three-years-old.

In September 1942 alone, some thirty-nine hundred people died, many elderly like Josef's mother. As was the usual custom, a small ceremony was held for the dead at the camp's mortuary after which the corpse was carried on a farm cart to the crematorium outside the walls. The ashes of the dead were kept there in numbered cardboard boxes. Family members hoped that once the ordeal in Theresienstadt passed, they would find their loved one's ashes and give them a decent burial. It was not to be. In late 1944, in an effort to destroy the evidence of what happened in Theresienstadt, the Germans ordered all ashes to be thrown into the nearby Eger River.

On October 30, 1944 the final deportation train left from Theresienstadt for Auschwitz. Of the 2,038 prisoners on board, 1,689 were immediatcly gassed.

Some months earlier, in April 1944, the Blechhammer concentration camp where Josef was imprisoned became a satellite camp of Auschwitz III-Monowitz and came under the control of the SS. All the women, including myself, were sent elsewhere. Later I learned that the male prisoners in the new Auschwitz complex at Blechhammer were tattooed. Josef was branded with the number 177231 on the outer side of his left forearm, a number he wore his entire life.

In September 1944, American bombers destroyed large parts of the plants of the Oberschlesische Hydrierwerke AG in Blechhammer and of the oil refinery in nearby Trzebinia. Josef and the other prisoners were marched to the partially destroyed factory. The SS then marched the prisoners back to the camp and assembled them. The officer-in-charge told them that, in all likelihood, one of them had communicated with the Americans, which in turn led to the bombing raid. To make sure that it would not happen again, the officer picked one prisoner and, as an example, hung him in front of Josef and the others.

Toward the end of the war, when it became clear the German army was trapped between the Soviets to the east and the advancing Allied troops from the west, the SS forced the inmates of the concentration camp to march westward. The evacuation from Blechhammer began on January 21, 1945. Josef and some four thousand other prisoners each got eight hundred grams of bread, a small portion of margarine, and artificial honey for their march. SS-Untersturmfuehrer Kurt Klipp, the Lagerleiter, or camp commandant, of Blechhammer led the death march. Meanwhile, the SS killed as many as two hundred prisoners who were ill or had attempted to hide.

Josef and the others walked from Blechhammer via Kole to Neustadt to Glucholazy to Neisse to Otmuchow. From there Josef marched to Zabkowice Slaskie to Schweidnitz and Strzegom. The SS shot approximately eight hundred prisoners, those who were not able to walk any longer, or who tried to flee. On February 2, 1945, Josef finally reached the Gross-Rosen concentration camp, which was originally established in 1940 as a sub camp of the Sachsenhausen concentration camp. The sub-camp was named for the nearby village of Gross-Rosen. Now called Rogoznica, the village is approximately forty miles southwest of Wroclaw in present-day western Poland.

Josef stayed in Gross-Rosen for five days. On February 6 or 7, 1945, Josef and three thousand other prisoners were transported to the

Buchenwald concentration camp. On the way, the train was attacked several times by Allied fighter planes, which caused many deaths. From Buchenwald, Josef was marched to Austria. It is believed the Jews were being taken to the Ebensee concentration camp. However, Josef and the others where liberated by the U.S. 11th Armored Division in Lebenau near Salzburg. At the time of his liberation, Josef came down with typhus. Thanks to the American Army, Josef was treated with medicine and recovered.

Afterward, Josef returned home to Kitzingen, Germany. He spent his time at the nearby Jewish cemetery of Roedelsee where his father Ferdinand was buried. To reach Roedelsee, which is thought to be over five hundred-years-old, a person had to travel a small lane through surrounding vineyards. In the cemetery, Josef replaced all the grave stones that had been knocked down during the war. The U.S. Army ordered the Germans living close by to help Josef. American soldiers remained at the cemetery until the work was completed.

Mimi, her father, Max Rubin, and sister, Blanka

Mimi's mother, Ernestine Rubin

Dela Reich informed my mother and me that Blanka was imprisoned with Dela's son, Fritz at the Sagan Concentration Camp in Germany

Mimi, Dela, and Blanka in Teschen, Czechoslovakia 1946

Mimi's sister, Blanka, after the war

Josef's friend Jim Schiller drove with him to Bayreuth from Heidelberg to pick me up after I was smuggled into Germany from Czechoslovakia

Josef's brother, Moritz Glückstein

*Josef working in the Jewish Cemetery of Roedelsee as
American soldiers and local Germans help*

*Mimi and Blanka's cousin Mark Drechsler, whose letter
they received in Nový Bohumín after liberation*

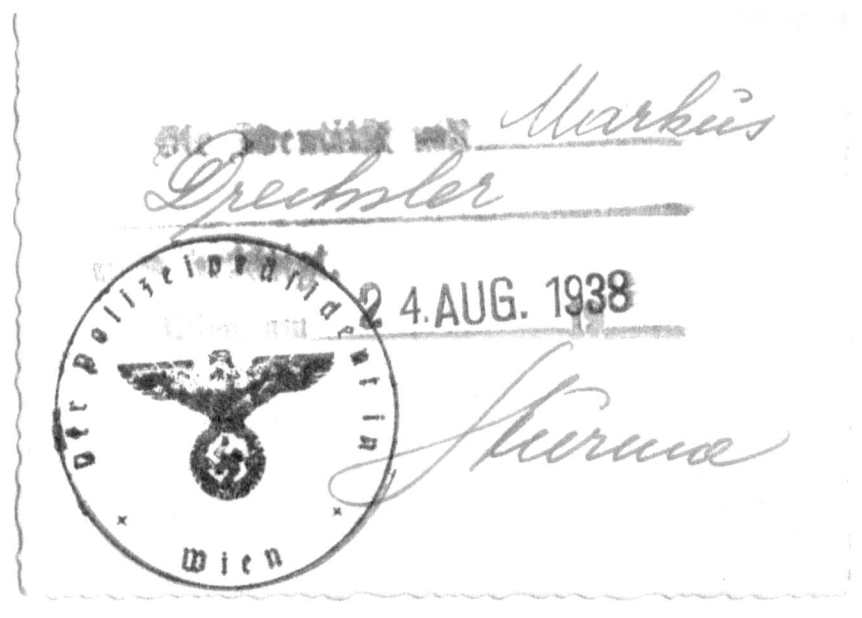

Mark Drechsler's transit card, issued in Austria on August 24, 1938

Stadtverwaltung Heidelberg

HEIDELBERG, GERMANY

R u b i n Mimi	29.9.23	☐ male/männlich
Last name/Name First name/Vorname	Date of birth Geburtsdatum	☒ fem./weiblich

Hauserstrasse 38	Unrra Team 622 K.Nr. Reg. 3357	
Local address/Jetzige Adresse	Identity card nr./Ausweisnummer	

Hausfrau	Angestellte	Czecks
Occupation or profession at present Derzeitiger Beruf bzw. Beschäftigung	Skill Erlernter Beruf	Claimed nationality Nationalität

Name and address of employer Name und Adresse des Arbeitgebers	1943 Date entered Germany Ankunftsdatum in Deutschland

10. Februar 1947
Resident of Heidelberg since
in Heidelberg seit

Stempel der Stadtverwaltung

15.2.47

Registered by:

Right index finger

*Mimi's registration card for Displaced Persons filed in
Heidelberg, Germany, after arrival in 1947*

44

Mimi and Josef's wedding day on March 11, 1947, in Heidelberg, Germany

Mimi and Josef's wedding photograph

Mimi's passport photo to the United States 1948

Joseph's passport photo to the United States 1948

Mimi with her children Fred and Ellen

Chapter Seven

Transferred to the Peterswaldau Concentration Camp

When Blechhammer was taken over by the SS as a sub-camp of Auschwitz in April 1944, I and all the other women were transported in April 1944 to Peterswaldau, a sub-camp of the Gross-Rosen concentration camp. At the time, Peterswaldau was in Germany. Today it is called Pieszyce, and it is located in south-western Poland. We travelled from Blechhammer by train and were lodged in the Peterswaldau Castle. The German guards in uniform were women. I would soon learn that the women guards were meaner and worse than the German men in the other camps. The women guards took away everything we had including our jewelry and allowed us to keep one dress and one piece of underwear. We were stripped naked and examined for skin disease. It was very humiliating.

We learned that the Germans had brought us to Peterswaldau to work in a nearby time bomb factory making the time pieces for the bombs. At 7:00 a.m. each morning the guards walked us to the factory. I noticed that the town was small with many private homes. I learned that the town's people had been ordered by the Germans to leave and the town was deserted. We worked at the factory until dinner time when the guards took us back to the castle and we ate. I remembered that the meal on Sunday wasn't bad. One meal was a tasty meat; however, we learned that it was horse meat and everyone got sick the next day.

Afterwards, we were transferred in town to what had been a Jewish-owned factory. I was thrilled to find Blanka and Delia there. In addition to those of us that been transferred from Blechhammer and other camps, one thousand Hungarian women joined us from the death camp at Auschwitz. These women had there their heads and hair shaved and wore jail type uniforms. The sleeping arrangements were terrible. I lived with one hundred thirty women in one room. The food was very bad. We were fed tomatoes and spinach soup that wasn't cooked properly. We could taste the ground's soil and there was no salt. Later the Germans included red salt that is given to animals.

I was assigned to a machine similar to a sewing machine in the time bomb factory. It required that I use my feet which became swollen. I suffered frostbite and when I could not walk, I spent three days in the infirmary. The weather was freezing cold. There was no warm water. We were allowed one shower a week on Saturday. It had to be completed quickly as the next group of women were on line to shower. Over time, we saw brick coals in the time bomb factory and agreed that each woman would take one or two and hide it in her clothes. We would use the coals to warm our rooms. Unfortunately, the Germans discovered the coals, and we were punished. We were required to be outdoors in the freezing cold for hours.

The hardships in Peterswaldau continued into 1945. During the evening of May 4, 1945, we saw from the windows that the Germans were leaving. We did not know what was happening. Shortly, thereafter, we were told by the Germans not to leave the Jewish-owned factory because the town was going to be destroyed. By noon of the next day,

May 5, 1945, a few women left the factory to see what was happening. They ran into inhabitants from a nearby concentration camp who explained that they had been liberated by the Soviet Union's Red Army. We now understood that the Germans had left because the allies were advancing. It also meant that the Soviet Red Army would soon be in Peterswaldau and we would be liberated. Later that day, on May 5, 1945, a large contingent of Russian soldiers and tanks entered Peterswaldau.

We were liberated.

Chapter Eight

Liberation from Peterswaldau
by the Soviet Red Army

One would expect that after the approximately one thousand other women and I were liberated at the Peterswaldau concentration camp by the Soviet Red Army, we would have had a joyful time, but we did not. To begin with, the Soviet Red Army stayed in Peterswaldau. The soldiers found wine and beer in the town and celebrated their entry into Germany. They were always drinking and often drunk. At night Russian soldiers would come into the women's rooms. A soldier would sit on the bed and tell the women that they needed to get friendlier and intimate. The soldier would say it was the least the women could do to thank him for the liberation. Some of the women complained to a Russian lieutenant who was Jewish. He spoke to the soldiers and placed armed guards at the entrance to protect the women. It didn't do any good. The persecution continued.

The women decided to take action. Blanka, Dela and I went out of the camp and into the town which had been evacuated. We found a villa that belonged to a pharmacist. We were happy to see a real bed and towels. We went to the pantry and had a nice breakfast. Blanka looked around the villa and downstairs found three bodies-the pharmacist, his wife, and their child. It appeared they had committed suicide. The bodies were taken out. Although we were scared when the doorbell rang, the Russians did not bother us.

A few weeks later the Red Cross arrived. It made arrangements to take the 1000 women prisoners home. Blanka, Dela, and I were told we would be driven to Prague, Czechoslovakia and from there we would be sent home. Finally the day of freedom arrived, and we boarded the large Red Cross truck. The civilian men of the Red Cross carried rifles and machine guns to protect themselves and us from any Germans that we might run into. After reaching Prague without incident, we were housed and told arrangements would be made to send us home. Since the major railroad station in Nový Bohumín was damaged, we decided to travel with Dela to her nearby home town of Teschen, which was part in Czechoslovakia and part in Poland.

The Red Cross arranged our travel to Teschen. Once there we leased a very nice furnished apartment. We didn't know what happened to the owners. In order to pay for the apartment, Blanka and I worked as typists in a Teschen police office. Dela, who was a much older woman, was unable to work. She remained in the apartment where she cooked and cleaned. A few weeks later, Blanka and I traveled by train for a short visit to Nový Bohumín. It had been five years since we had last been there. During that time my father, mother, and grand mother had all died. Blanka and I had been in ghettoes and concentration camps. It was a miracle that we had survived.

Once we arrived in Nový Bohumín, we ran into a few young men that we knew. They had survived the war in the French Foreign Legion and had returned home. Blanka and I went to our grandparents' building where we had lived. The house looked much older and in need of extensive repair. We did not know anyone who lived there. Afterwards,

Blanka and a lawyer went to the town office to regain ownership of my grandparent's apartment building. They were told that the building was rundown and no one had paid taxes while the Germans occupied it. It was explained that the taxes due were more than the building was worth. Without monies to pay the rent and undertake repairs, we had no choice but to forget taking back ownership. It was sad and disappointing.

Before returning to Teschen, Blanka and I stopped at the small store near the apartment building. The store sold dairy and other dairy products. The woman in the store recognized Blanka and me. Surprisingly, she had a letter for us. It had been sent to our apartment building, but when it could not be delivered the store held it. You can imagine how excited Blanka and I were to know that a letter was waiting for us. The letter was from our cousin Max Drechsler, who was the son of my father's sister. Max was able to get to the United States from Belgium in 1940. He worked for his uncle, a furrier, in New York. Max had written the letter to my family as the war came to a close to learn whether we had survived.

Afterward, we left Nový Bohumín for the last time and returned to Teschen where Blanka, Dela, and I started building new lives. During that time, we became acquainted with a few Jewish people that lived in the building, including a doctor and a pharmacist. Meanwhile, my cousin Max Drechsler tried to help Blanka and me move to the United States, but he was unable to convince his uncle to provide the necessary affidavit and guarantee of financial support.

One day in 1946, I received a letter from a woman that I had met in the Blechhammer concentration camp. Her name was Sosza Bond and she was Polish. After the liberation, she had spent time in a displaced person's camp in Munich, Germany. Sosza wrote to tell me that Josef Glückstein was alive and living in Heidelberg, Germany. Shortly, thereafter I received a letter from him. Josef had received a book from a Jewish organization that listed concentration camp survivors and saw my name. He suggested that I travel to Heidelberg and we would get married.

I wrote Josef and told him that I would come. However, leaving Czechoslovakia was a major problem because after the war ended the country had come under the domination of the Soviet Union. Soviet Red Army troops occupied Czechoslovakia and did not allow Czech citizens to leave the country at the border crossings. In 1947, I learned of a Jewish organization in Prague that smuggled Jews into Germany. I contacted the group and made arrangements to travel illegally into Germany. I said goodbye to Blanka and Dela and left Teschen by myself. I took the train to Prague, where some young Jewish men and women met me. I stayed in their apartment for a few days.

Shortly thereafter, a few Jewish men who were also travelling to Germany joined me. We boarded a car and a member of the Jewish organization drove. It was winter and the weather was cold and it had snowed. To avoid the Russian guards at the border points, we travelled into Germany across Czech fields covered by ice and snow. Once we were in Germany, I was driven to Bayreuph and the home of Karl Demerer who I remembered as the "camp elder" at Blechhammer. Miraculously, Karl had survived with his wife and two children.

The arrangement was for Josef to drive from Heidelberg, a city in Baden-Württemberg that lies on the river Neckar, to Bayreuth and pick me up. A friend of Josef's named Jim Schiller would accompany him. (After Josef was liberated in Austria, he went to Belgium to find any of the prisoners he'd met before he had been sent by the Germans to Blechhammer. While in Belgium, he and Jim became friends and they both went to Heidelberg.)) On the way to Bayreuth by car, Josef and Jim hit bad weather. As they got closer, they ended up in a ditch. Unable to get the car out, they found a German farmer who helped. Josef gave him a pair of slippers which were difficult to obtain after the war. Finally they arrived at the Demerer home. The next morning Josef, Jim, and I left for Heidelberg. We arrived there on February 10, 1947.

We lived with Josef's brother Moritz and his wife at Haeusserstrasse 38. Moritz had survived a concentration camp in Russia. Josef also had two other brothers who had left Germany before the Nazi onslaught: David lived in England and Abraham in Palestine. Sadly, like my mother and father Josef's six other brothers and sisters were killed by the Nazis.

Chapter Nine

The Story of Konrad Schweser

As a Czechoslovakian citizen and foreigner now in post-war Germany, I had to file a Registration Card for Displaced Persons with the city authorities in Heidelberg on February 15, 1947. At the time, Josef's brother Moritz wrote a letter to the United States military authorities on the courage and decency of a German camp official named Konrad Schweser. After the war ended, Schweser was arrested by the Americans and placed in a military prison in Ochsenfurt.

Before I arrived in Heidelberg, Moritz sent a letter to the Military Government in Ochsenfurt on July 23, 1946. His letter told the Americans how Schweser placed his own life in jeopardy to save the lives of the Jews, including Moritz's, under his jurisdiction. The remarkable story of Konrad Schweser contain in the letter has been translated from German to English and will be found in the appendix.

Moritz's letter to the Military Government led to Konrad Schweser being freed. In 1965, Schweser was honored as a non-Jew who saved Jews at personal risk during the Holocaust in the ""Righteous Among the Nations"" memorial at Yad Vashem, Israel's official memorial of the Jewish victims of the Holocaust.

Elie Wiesel wrote about the courage of people like Schweser. "In those times, there was darkness everywhere. In heaven and on earth, all the gates of compassion seemed to have been closed. The killer killed, and the Jews died and the outside world adopted an attitude either of complicity or of indifference. Only a few had the courage to care. These few men and women were vulnerable, afraid, and helpless. What made them different from their fellow citizens? …Why were there so few? … Let us remember: What hurts the victim most is not the cruelty of the oppressor but the silence of the bystander… Let us not forget, after all, there is always a moment when moral choice is made … And so we must know these good people who helped Jews during the Holocaust. We must learn from them, and in gratitude and hope, we must remember them."

Although Conrad Schweser passed away some time ago, I am pleased to still be in contact with his elderly daughter who lives in Germany.

Chapter Ten

Josef and I Marry on March 11, 1947
in Heidelberg, Germany

Before my departure for Germany, my sister Blanka and I met Dela's cousin, a man named Fritz Kestel. He was a Jew from Bielsko, Poland. Coincidentally, Dela's deceased son was also named Fritz. During the war Fritz Kestel, his wife, and two sons, Theodore and George, were imprisoned in Russia. Fritz's wife died there, but he and his two sons survived. After the war, toward the end of 1946, Fritz sent the boys to England, and he started to look for any family members that may have survived the Holocaust. Using the services of the International Red Cross, he was happy to find his cousin Dela Reich alive and visited her in Teschen, where Blanka and I were introduced to him for the first time.

After I immigrated to Germany, Blanka and Fritz Kestel married. They along with Fritz's two sons, who had returned from England, lived in Poland. However, in January 1950, Blanka, Fritz, and the boys went to Israel and began a new life in the city of Haifa. In 1956, they persuaded Dela to emigrate from Czechoslovakia and join them. Sadly, after arriving in Israel, Dela had an appendicitis attack and died. She was buried in the old cemetery in Haifa.

Our son Ferdinand, named after Josef's father, was born in the St. Elisabeth Private Clinic in Heidelberg on February 21, 1948. Overtime, it became too difficult for Josef and me to remain in Germany. We were always reminded of our personal losses and the history of Heidelberg, and that made it difficult to forget what happened.

We learned that during Kristallnacht in November 1938, the Nazis burned down synagogues at two locations in Heidelberg. The next day, the systematic deportation of Jews started, and one hundred fifty Jews were sent to the Dachau concentration camp. On October 22, 1940, during the ""Wagner Buerckel event,"" six thousand local Jews, including two hundred eighty from Heidelberg, were deported to a concentration camp. With the war coming to an end on March 29, 1945 the German Army left the city. After destroying three arches of the old bridge, they destroyed the other more modern bridge that crossed a little further downstream. The blown-up bridges proved no obstacle for the U.S. Army forces (3rd Infantry, 7th Army), which entered Heidelberg on March 30, 1945. Heidelberg was handed over without any resistance by the civilian population.

It has been theorized by some that Heidelberg escaped bombing in the Second World War because the U.S. Army wanted to use the city as a garrison. In fact, as Heidelberg was neither an industrial center nor a transport hub, there was felt to be nothing worth bombing there. Instead, Allied air raids focused extensively on the nearby industrial cities of Mannheim and Ludwigshafen.

In 1948, Josef and I decided to leave Germany and come to the United States. We contacted the American Jewish Joint Distribution Committee, which was referred to as Joint. They informed us that they would pay for the cost of transportation to the United States and help to cover some expenses upon arrival. However, we had to wait until Ferdinand was at least four months old before we could travel. Meanwhile, we made the necessary arrangements.

As a German national, Josef obtained a Temporary Travel Document in lieu of a passport from the Military Government for Germany, which consisted of France, Britain, and America. He chose to use the name Glueckstein, rather than Glückstein, because the German umlaut above the "u" was not used in English. Finally, we left Bremerhaven for New York aboard the S.S. Marine Flasher on July 16, 1948. Our baggage included two trunks, five handbags, and two boxes. I was twenty-six years of age, Josef was thirty-five, and Ferdinand (we would later call him Fred) was four months old. The ship's manifest of passengers travelling to the United States included men, women, and children that were Germans, Hungarians, Latvians, Austrians, and Yugoslavs; some were categorized as Stateless.

Aboard ship, I shared living quarters with another woman who also had a young baby. Our accommodations had cribs for our children. Josef slept further below ship with other men. After the Marine Flasher was at sea, the weather got cold. I remember the women opening their luggage and taking out their winter coats to keep themselves warm. We ate at table no. eight on the B Deck Dining Room. After ten days at sea, we arrived in New York City on July 26, 1948. The weather was hot, with the temperature in the mid-90s. Neither Josef nor I spoke English, and we had little money.

My cousin, Max Drechsler, met us at the pier. With other Holocaust survivors aboard the ship, we spent the first two weeks of our arrival at a hotel on 103th Street in Manhattan. During that time we were expected to find housing. We eventually moved to Max's apartment building in the Bronx, where we leased an apartment at 1011 Sheridan Avenue off the Grand Concourse. On June 26, 1950, my second child, a daughter, was born in the Bronx. We named her Ellen.

Josef's first job in America was in a pocketbook factory in Brooklyn. The owner, who was Austrian, paid Josef approximately eighty-five cents an hour for fixing his company's pocketbooks. When our daughter Ellen was born, Josef asked the owner for a raise. It was granted, and his hourly salary was raised five cents to ninety cents an hour. Needing a higher salary to support a wife and two children, Josef left the pocketbook factory and took a job at a feather factory in Manhattan. He boxed feathers for shipment. The job required that Josef work night from 7:00 p.m. to 8:00 a.m. Being a Jewish-owned company, the factory was closed on Fridays and Saturdays for religious observance.

Meanwhile, Josef learned that Paul Fromm, the owner of the wine company that had employed him in Germany years earlier, now had a wine-importing company in America. The new company, Geeting and Fromm Importers, was located in Chicago. Josef had been very good as a wine representative for Mr. Fromm, and he knew it would be a great opportunity to once again work for him. Josef wrote him a letter on July 7, 1949.

Mr. Fromm responded as follows:

Dear Josef:

Thank you for your letter on July 4th. It certainly has given me genuine pleasure to learn that you have arrived with your family, and established a new home in the United States.

I knew also that you and Moritz have survived the Nazi years. With all the tragedies the Jews had to suffer at the hands of the Nazis, we all should be so much more grateful for the few miracles that have happened.

At present we have no opening in our sales department as all our territories are distributed, but changes may take place, and you may be assured that I would think of you if a possibility for joining our organization would come up.

Please keep me advised of any change of address. In September I intend to come to New York, and then would like to meet you.

With best regards and kindest wishes, I am
Sincerely yours,
Paul Fromm

Despite the encouraging letter, Mr. Fromm did not come to New York and although some additional correspondence passed between them both, no opportunity was offered to Josef. It was another disappointment to deal with.

In those early days in New York, I always remember Josef saying he waited for the day when he had $45.50 in the bank each month to pay for the rent. Overtime, he took another job in sales for a company which he held for the rest of his career. When the children were older, I took a part-time job. Although it was difficult and challenging, Josef and I worked hard and succeeded in making a good life in our new country.

Afterword

As I related the story of my life before and during World War II, I often thought about the deaths of my mother, father, and grandmother. Before Josef's death in 1999, I know that he always thought about the loss of his mother, sisters, and brothers in the camps. For many years, I did not want to talk about my experiences in the Holocaust. But the years are moving ahead quickly and the time to tell my story has come.

Melissa Müller, a journalist who lives in Munich and Vienna, wrote *Anne Frank: The Biography* in 1998. It was published in Germany under the title *Das Mädchen Anne Frank* and translated into English. Ms. Muller wrote: "The historian Yehuda Bauer has said that historical research cannot rely on theoretical analysis alone; it requires as well the telling of true stories. A storyteller has a greater chance of reaching people than a theorist, and I have tried to tell the story of Anne Frank, her family, and her circle of friends in such a way that people will listen. My listeners, I hope, will reflect on the crimes of the Nazis, on the social conditions that proved fertile ground for their unspeakable horrors."

I hope my true story will reach both young and old. It is my fervent desire that my experience will keep alive the memory of the millions of innocent men, women, and children that died in the German concentration camps during the 1930s and 1940s.

Note to reader: Mimi Rubin Glueckstein died on April 4, 2016.

Appendix

Konrad Schweser

Moriitz Glückstein
From Kitzingen A.M.
At present Heidelberg
Heauserstr. 38

To the Military Government
Ochsenfurt A.M.

Re.: Schweser, Konrad, Ochsenfurt, at present inmate at the
district court prison.

I respectfully request to release Mr. Schweser from the prison.
The reason of my request is as follows:

I am a Jew. I was born on January 15, 1902 at Kitzingen/Main.
In the year 1939 I was discharged from my work place due to the
fact that I belonged to the Jewish religion. I was in Bingen at that
time. Since I had infringed against an exceptional law at the time,
I was to be punished and expatriated. In order to avoid execution

or punishment which automatically meant imprisonment in a concentration camp, I ran away to Kattowitz (Poland). This was in the middle of July 1939. There the beginning of the war caught up with me. I was arrested by the Germans and brought to a camp.

From there I was able to run away to the Russian occupied part of Poland. In 1941 I was again arrested by the Germans. I was taken to a camp in Stupki near Teplik (Ukraine). This is where, in 1942, I met Mr. Konrad Schweser.

Mr. Schweser was a paramilitary master sergeant for the O.T. (Organization Todt which was responsible for the construction projects such as highways, railways, and ammunition factories) and worked as a lineman. Mr. Schweser also had to take care of a number of camps, one of which was Teplik. His duties included overseeing daily food rations and to regulate labor details. Schweser lived at Teplik.

Schweser took care of all camp inmates in an exemplary manner, which made him known as "father" by all. Jews in the surrounding camps were eager to be transferred to Schweser. When Schweser was near-by the camp inmates knew "now, even though the SS is present, nothing could happen to us." Schweser saw to it that no local citizen or Jew was ever beaten or ill treated. If Germans or people from the Ukraine ever made an encroachment against the Jews, he was right there to stop it. In two cases (those of Geiger and Steinborn) he filed a complaint. Both had robbed Jews of their belongings. Each was convicted and received imprisonment of two years and one and one-half years respectively.

Wherever Schweser was, the Jews had to fear nothing. One time when Schweser was on vacation everybody was down and out and feared for the worst. We all counted the days and could hardly wait for him to return. His return was greeted with relief. Contrary to the ration regulation Schweser, though he was prohibited, made sure that we received monthly a substantial provision of food out of the military stock. In addition we received bread for the ill, meat, marmalade, sugar oil, salt etc. as well as peas, beans, lentils cornmeal and millet. Out of personal experience, I know that if you went to him and told him that the people are hungry, he would distribute one hundred-fifty to two hundred loaves of bread. According to orders, bread was to be baked with millet meal; however, Schweser would not allow this and ordered that wheat flour would be used.

Once we had a typhoid epidemic. In such cases, the SS would use a radical procedure. All camp inmates would be shot and the camp burned down to the ground. In order to save the people, Schweser thought hard and long on what he could do to keep the epidemic a secret. He took all the healthy at once and deposited them in a cloister. The infected ones he moved from a lice infected dormitory into a clean neighboring building.

He also organized a disinfection apparatus to ward off additional cases of typhus. In order to keep the truth from the SS, he was able to camouflage the daily labor detail. The vaccine was scarce and only available for the Germans. Nevertheless, Schweser had the Jews vaccinated three times where and whenever it was possible. He himself was only vaccinated once, and therefore became a victim of his own public caretaking and contracted typhus. During the convalescence time of the illness, he took care of the camp residents like a father. He made sure they had additional white bread available. In addition, he made sure that they received other rations such as milk, butter, eggs, meat, etc.

From experience, I know that Schweser saved the lives of at least forty-four Jews most of whose names and addresses I can provide. I myself thank Schweser for saving my life. Here are some of the events:

One day Schweser had a wooden crate made and in it had bread delivered to the camp, After empting the crate Mr. Schweser had left orders that a Jewess by the name of Scheiner climb into the crate. The crate with Mrs. Scheiner left the camp. This is how Mrs. Scheiner was saved and today lives in Bucharest. About six weeks ago, I talked with her.

The SS was told to kill all the children. Schweser hid six of the Jewish children near his apartment and eventually had them transported out of the camp in the same manner as Mrs. Scheiner, whose child was among the six. They were also brought to Romania. I myself talked to those children at a later point at the Jewish Children's Home at Berschad/ Romania.

I was saved by Schweser in the following manner: he ordered a horse and carriage and made sure I received proper identification. After that I was to drive sunflower kernels to a mill for processing into oil. Schweser had made arrangements for me to get in touch with a smuggler. Schweser sent along a confidante who was to bring back the horse and carriage. That is how I escaped. He ordered me to call him at once in case anything should happen on the way to freedom, like imprisonment. He would then fetch me by car if necessary.

A woman and her daughter were saved the following way: their names are Mrs. Lande (mother) and Ginzia Lande (daughter). At present, they live in Bucharest, Stupinei 34D. One night the camp Treplik was surrounded by the SS. The police and Ukrainian

Military Police (Miliz) for the camp were to be transferred elsewhere. Schweser sent his secretary with a note to the on-duty watchman of the "Miliz" that Mrs. Lande and daughter were to come to him to take care of his laundry. They both came. Schweser hid them and later made it possible for them to escape across the border. However, they were caught. They asked to be brought to Schweser and he, deceiving the police, hid them again. Through a confidante, both were smuggled across the border.

Schweser had built a partition on top of a truck. This truck, with a Russian driver, was to go to Cernowitz to fetch material and gasoline. In the partition he put five Jews and made their escape possible. It was the family Schorr at present in Medias Romania. In another instance he had a tailor shop built. There the two Jewish tailors and their wives were now able to outfit themselves with proper clothes and flee.

Quite a number of similar cases can be brought forward. In every case Schweser risked his life and did not ever ask for anything in return. The Jews did not have anything themselves and would have been embarrassed to offer Schweser something for his humanitarian efforts. On the contrary, he had nothing but problems. While I was there the SS wanted him to be court-martialed in Winnizza/Ukraine for assisting the escape of Jews in two cases. After my escape, I found out that the SS tried to court-martial him for additional cases, one of which was for helping me escape and another for distributing rations out of the military depot for Jews.

Schweser, in addition, helped Jews financially out of his pocket.

To help the sick Jews, Schweser tried any which way he could to get the necessary medication. Even though it was not easy to do he was successful. I remember a case in my presence when a Jewess came and asked Schweser for an insulin injection for her very ill father. He immediately got dressed and went with me and the girl to the pharmacy. He received the medication which normally Jews were not able to get.

I can go on and on with many more details which will distinguish Schweser for his humanitarian efforts. Schweser tried to save many lives during difficult times and he was successful in many cases, even as he put his own life in jeopardy. He is entitled to be separated from the masses of the German people as one who risked his own life for humanitarian efforts. This is the reason why I plead for his release from prison. Schweser did so much for human society that he surely deserves all our support. He does not belong in prison; rather, he needs to be returned to society.

All the many people he saved will give praise to him all over the globe. The name of "Schweser" brings a good sound to many not only in Poland, Romania, and Ukraine, but moreover around the globe. Many people cannot wait to thank him personally as soon as this is possible.

I plead with you once more to release Mr. Schweser. I do this as interpreter for all the many people whose lives he saved.

July 23, 1946

Moritz Glückstein
From Kitzingen
At present Heidelberg
Heauserstr. 38

Moritz's letter to the Military Government led to Konrad Schweser being freed.

Index